Beginner's Guide to Selling on Ebay!

By
Ann Eckhart

Table of Contents

INTRODUCTION

I have been selling on Ebay since 2005, and I've been educating others about selling on the site for nearly as long. I have written numerous books on Ebay topics such as where to find items to sell, how to ship packages through Ebay, how to start a home-based Ebay business, and more. However, this book is far and away my best seller, because it teaches people EXACTLY how to sell on Ebay!

While it's easy to tell people just to log on to Ebay.com and follow their instructions to list items for sale, those who have no experience with the site often want someone to walk them through the process. And that is what I will be doing in this book, walking you through step-by-step through everything you need to do to get started selling on Ebay!

This book is strictly geared for beginners, people who have never bought or sold on Ebay before, or who have done so without much success. I will be going over the basics, such as what exactly Ebay and PayPal are, if they are safe (a big concern for many people), and why you should even sell online at all. I'll walk you through creating your first listings, how to figure shipping, and how to package up orders. In addition, I'll share tips and tricks on how to deal with problems, communicate with customers, and manage your Ebay account.

Ebay offers you the best opportunity to get top dollar for your items. While you might get a quarter for an old CD at a garage sale, you may be able to get $10 or more for it on Ebay. In fact, once you know how to sell on Ebay, you'll be able to scrap together cash in a pinch. If an unexpected bill pops up, you'll be able to pull some items from your closet to sell in order to pay that bill fast. Knowing how to sell on Ebay provides you with an added layer of financial security; I truly believe that schools should teach kids how to sell online as it's something that anyone can do at any time!

Ebay is a unique marketplace with its own special learning curve to master. However, with this book, as well as with a little time and practice, you'll be selling on Ebay and making money in no time! I know that Ebay can see overwhelming at first (even I was scared to use it before I started my account), but once you have a few listings under your belt and have shipped out a couple of orders, you'll realize how easy it actually is!

CHAPTER 1

WHAT EXACTLY IS EBAY?

Ebay debuted in 1995 as an online classified ads marketplace. It offered people all over America the ability to list items they had for sale and to sell them to customers across the country. When Ebay first started, it was an online auction site; people put their items up for auction and customers bid on them. The highest bidder won the item, paid the seller through Ebay's payment system (PayPal), and then the seller shipped them their merchandise. In the beginning, customers were also able to bypass PayPal altogether and mail checks to sellers, and sometimes they even sent cash!

Ebay quickly expanded to sellers and buyers worldwide. While auctions and antiques remain what the site is known for, these days sellers large and small sell both new and used products through Ebay at what is called "Fixed Price"; i.e. the seller sets the price and there is no bidding. I sometimes miss the days when you could start every item at a 99-cent auction and watch the bidding go up and up! However, those days are long gone except for very rare, in-demand collectibles. Nowadays, Ebay is mainly a "buy it now" shopping site.

I have been selling on Ebay since 2005, and I have shipped items to every corner of the globe. When I first started selling on Ebay, it was one of the few online shopping websites, meaning you could sell nearly anything on it. Today, Ebay competes with Amazon for the top marketplace spot, and nearly every retailer has their own website. And sites like Poshmark, Etsy and Mercari are only making the online selling landscape even more crowded.

Competition is much more competitive than when I first started selling online. Therefore, the types of items that sell and the method in which they sell have changed greatly. Now many sellers turn to Amazon to sell their new goods, while Ebay is more centered on secondhand items. However, while things may not always sell as fast as they once did on Ebay, you can sell almost anything there, new or used. And more and more companies are expanding on to Ebay with their new goods. Today the sky's the limit for what you can sell on Ebay, whether new or used.

Despite the competition, Ebay is still the number one site for individuals to sell their items to people across the globe. Ebay continues to expand and improve, giving sellers like me confidence that they will be around for years to come. With nearly two hundred million registered Ebay users, there are still plenty of opportunities to make money on Ebay.

CHAPTER 2

WHY SELL ON EBAY?

Why sell your items on Ebay as opposed to a garage sale or consignment shop? Hands down, you will get the most money for your items on Ebay! As I mentioned earlier, there are nearly 200 million registered Ebay users, meaning there are 200 million more chances for you to sell your items.

Let's say you have a rare collectible. While only a handful of people will come to a garage sale or enter a consignment shop, on Ebay, your item is available for purchase to the millions of Ebay account holders. You only need to find that one buyer to get top dollar for your item. The chances of that buyer coming to your garage sale are slim to none; but the odds are much better that the customer will find you on Ebay.

While Ebay does charge fees for both listing items and selling them (called Listing and Final Value Fees), these charges are much less than an auction house or consignment shop would take. With a little bit of work on your end, you can get the most money possible for your items. I have items in my store that I'd be lucky to get a quarter for at a garage sale that sell for $20 and up on Ebay.

Learning to sell on Ebay provides you with a certain level of financial protection. Once you know how to sell on Ebay, you can sell your unwanted items for top dollar at any time, raising cash quickly if the need arises. You can earn a couple hundred dollars fast by selling your stuff at a garage sale; or you might be able to rack in a few thousand in a couple of weeks on Ebay! Most people who sell on Ebay got their start by selling their unwanted possessions from their own homes. And once they were hooked on selling off their own stuff, they started searching thrift stores and garage sales for more items to flip.

CHAPTER 3

WHAT IS PAYPAL?

PayPal is Ebay's payment system. Think of it as Ebay's own bank. When you create a PayPal account, you link it to your bank account and/or your debit/credit card. When someone buys something from you, they pay you through Ebay so that you and your customer never have to exchange sensitive payment information. It also means you, as a seller, don't have to set up any sort of third-party credit card processing system. All payments are handled directly through Ebay and PayPal.

Here is an example: Let's say you have a book for sale on Ebay for $10. Someone in England buys it. Ebay sends the buyer a notice that they have agreed to purchase your book and instructs them to pay you via PayPal. The buyer follows the link given to them by Ebay, logs into THEIR own personal PayPal account, and pays the money owed. Perhaps they already have funds in their PayPal account to pay with; or they may have their PayPal account linked to their credit card. Regardless, the money from their account is transferred BY EBAY into YOUR account. You and the buyer never exchange any payment details; it is all handled by Ebay through PayPal. Once the buyer pays, the money shows up in YOUR PayPal account. You then ship the item through Ebay, and the money for the shipping label automatically comes out of PayPal. After you've shipped your orders, you can then withdraw the remaining funds into your personal bank account or leave it in PayPal to pay with items you yourself are buying online.

Many people are nervous about selling on Ebay and accepting payments through PayPal because they worry their personal information as well as their banking information isn't safe. Ebay and PayPal have been around for over two decades and have handled billions of transactions. As long as you guard your log in information the same way you protect your other banking passwords, you will be safe using PayPal.

In fact, PayPal is much safer than having people send you personal checks, which could bounce. It's even safer than handling your own credit card processing as you don't have to worry about dealing with potentially fraudulent cards. Since PayPal handles all responsibility for processing payments, they assume all of the risks. You are then free to pay and be paid via your PayPal account without having to deal directly with anyone!

UPDATE: In 2019, Ebay started to roll out their own payment system, called Managed Payments, which allows shoppers to check out directly with Ebay, eliminating the need for PayPal. Sellers will still be able to offer PayPal as an option, buy Ebay will handle direct credit and debit card payments for sellers. This program is still in the early stages of testing and won't be site wide for a couple of years. Note that I myself have NOT opted into the new payment system as there are a lot of glitches in these early stages. I'm still using PayPal exclusively for payments. However, new sellers are now being required to use the

Managed Payments system; so, if you haven't yet set up your Ebay account, you'll likely be in the Managed Payments program when you do.

CHAPTER 4

THE TOOLS & SKILLS YOU NEED TO HAVE TO SELL ON EBAY

There are certain skills and tools you will need to have in order to successfully sell on Ebay. I have watched far too many new people attempt to sell on Ebay without having first mastered these skills or acquired the necessary equipment. Needless to say, their Ebay selling careers were short lived. While it's tempting to jump head-first into selling online, a lot more goes into using Ebay than just having products to sell.

Equipment: The first pieces of equipment you must have in order to sell on Ebay are a **computer**, **printer** and **camera**. You also need **internet access** and a strong working knowledge of computers. While you don't need to know programming or html code to sell online, Ebay is an online business that is run via the internet using computers; so not only do you need to be comfortable with the internet, computers, and printers, you also have to actually own these tools.

Having a computer set up may seem completely obvious to most people, but I can't tell you how many times I have been approached by someone asking me about how they can sell on Ebay…. without a computer! Or by people who have no idea how to even use one!

If you don't already have a computer, printer, and/or smart phone/digital camera, start shopping the sales and looking for a basic model; you can get a beginning set up of equipment for anywhere from $500 to $1000. I currently use an HP laptop, an HP LaserJet printer, and my iPhone camera to take photos (although I started with a basic Canon point-and-shoot camera).

If you aren't familiar with computers or if you need to brush up on your skills, look for free or low-cost computer classes in your area at the library, community college, or recreational center. Many colleges these days also offer "how to sell on Ebay classes"; while reading books is a great way to learn, sometimes it is also helpful to have someone help you in person. Check your local library or community college to see what beginner computer classes they may offer.

Reliable internet access is critical to selling on Ebay. I pay $50 a month for high-speed internet access. Most phone and cable companies now offer internet services, including modems so that you can have wireless access. Call around to the internet providers in your area and ask about any packages or specials they have for new customers. Be careful about getting locked into a long-term contract, however; and be sure you are aware of any price increases that will take place once the introductory special is over. Trust me when I say that high-speed interest is worth the price if you want to sell a significant number of items on Ebay; you'll easily be able to afford the cost with the additional sales you'll make!

Space: Not only do you need an office space for your computer equipment, you also need to have room to store your inventory and shipping supplies. I currently have a basement dedicated to my Ebay stock, but at one time I had it all in a spare bedroom. And even if you don't plan on running a full-scale Ebay business, you are going to need a place to keep the items you are selling, whether it's a spare closet or the corner of a room. While most of my Ebay items are in my basement, Ebay inventory and shipping materials tend to find their ways into all parts of my home.

Oh, did I just mention the shipping materials? From boxes and envelopes to tape and packing paper, the supplies you need to keep on hand to ship your Ebay items can easily fill a closet on their own. I actually have several shelving units and a desk dedicated to my Ebay shipping supplies. I'll talk more about the specific shipping supplies you need coming up.

I also have a separate table in my office for my digital scale as well as a dedicated space set up for taking photographs. I've invested in enclosure cards that go into every package that thank customers for their order. The "stuff" I need to run my Ebay business almost takes up as much space as my inventory! But many sellers start out with one corner of a room and a closest; so, if you are short on space but have the desire to sell online, you'll find a way to make it work.

Does all of this sound like too much money? Do you hate technology and have zero desire to learn about computers? Are you realizing that you just don't have the space to store inventory and shipping boxes? Then selling on Ebay may not be for you. However, if you have or can obtain the needed equipment, read on!

Digital Scale: One item you MUST have if you are going to sell on Ebay is a digital scale to weigh packages. You can buy digital scales for around $20 on Ebay, and they are also sold at office supply stores and on Amazon.

You don't need a fancy model, just a scale that weighs ounces and pounds. I have had the same digital scale for over seven years now; it's a small investment you MUST make if you are going to ship your Ebay orders yourself. If you aren't willing to purchase a digital scale for your Ebay shipping, then you should stop reading this book and resign yourself to hauling all of your packages to the Post Office. And running to the Post Office every day is not only time-consuming and expensive in terms of gas and wear and tear on your car, but you'll pay more in postage at the Post Office than you will if you print your shipping labels online (more on this later in the book).

I have encountered many sellers over the years who sell on Ebay without a scale. They estimate the shipping, overcharging customers in some cases (and getting negative feedback) or undercharging and losing money. Or they take all items to the Post Office BEFORE listing them to get a weight, list them, and then go BACK to the Post Office for postage after they sell. That, to me, is a HUGE waste of time and gas money!

I also see many sellers charging all customers one flat rate for shipping, which can be a big mistake if you sell many different sizes of items. Buyers come to Ebay for deals, and the shipping charges factor into that. As I stated above, charging one flat rate will result in overcharging

13

some customers and undercharging others. However, if you offer CALCULATED SHIPPING, the buyer pays the actual shipping cost based on the weight of the package and the zip code it is going to. If you have a digital scale on hand, using calculated shipping is a breeze. I will talk more about shipping later on in this book.

Other sellers offer "free" shipping, padding the cost of the item into their estimated shipping charge. While offering free shipping is a smart move for lightweight items (for instance, if you have a piece of jewelry that weighs 2-ounces, you can easily offer free shipping and absorb the $3 it will cost to ship), it can backfire on heavier items as buyers know when a seller has inflated the price of an item to cover shipping. You don't want to give the appearance that you are making money from the shipping costs and risk getting negative feedback.

Changing one flat postage rate really only works if you sell one size of items, say postcards or bras. I sell everything from makeup and books to figurines and dishes; so, the one-size-fits-all shipping charges do not work for me.

Instead of guessing the postage costs or running back and forth to the Post Office, you can save time and money by easily printing your shipping labels from home....and a digital scale makes that possible!

Boxes & Envelopes: You can't just stick a label directly on a book and send it in the mail (although, sadly, some new sellers do this). Shipping requires shipping supplies, and that means shipping boxes and envelopes.

The great thing about the United States Postal Service (USPS) is that they offer **FREE Priority Mail shipping boxes** (I will be talking a lot more about Priority Mail and the other forms of shipping services coming up). While Priority Mail is a great option for shipping most packages, you will need other forms of packaging for Media Mail, First Class Mail and Parcel Select, as well as for international shipments. Basically, you need two forms of shipping boxes/envelopes: Priority Mail boxes and envelopes for Priority Mail, and **plain boxes and envelopes** for Media Mail, First Class Mail, and Parcel Select.

Before you run out and buy new shipping boxes and envelopes, check around your house to see what you have on hand. Plain cardboard boxes, manila envelopes, and bubble mailers can all be used for non-Priority mail. If you already have items on hand you that you will be listing on Ebay, look them over to determine the packaging you need. Perhaps you are only going to sell books, for which bubble mailers and sturdy boxes are enough. However, if you only plan to sell large items, you don't need to worry about stocking up on envelopes.

I keep a wide variety of boxes and envelopes on hand. While I utilize the free Priority Mail boxes and bubble mailers from the Post Office, I do invest in nice shipping boxes and poly mailers that I purchase online. Ebay and Amazon both have great deals on boxes and mailers.

However, because I have been selling on Ebay for years and am set up as a business, these are items I can buy and then deduct as business expenses. If you are just starting out, use what you already have on hand; and don't be shy about asking your friends and family for any boxes they may have. With more and more people shopping online, many people have accumulated cardboard boxes they are desperate to get rid of. I save every box that I myself get a shipment in. I often order online from Amazon, and their boxes are a great size for shipping oddly shaped items such as board games.

If you are using repurposed boxes, be sure to use a marker to black out any writing on the outside of the box. You want to neatly cover up any company names or other information on the outside. I always pick up the thick black Sharpies when I see them on sale for this very purpose.

Also, do not wrap your boxes in brown wrapping paper. This is something I see a lot of new Ebay sellers do, but it is completely unnecessary. Not only is it a waste of time and money, the Post Office actually prefers that you do NOT wrap your boxes as the paper can become lodged in the sorting machines.

Packing Materials: You can't just throw an item into a box and ship it with no packing materials to buffer it inside of the box (well, you CAN, as I have seen many new sellers do; but you shouldn't). You need to WRAP up your items to protect them inside of the box. Again, since I have an established Ebay business, I invest in recycled **packing paper** to wrap up the items. However, I then use newspapers to further protect the item. Do NOT wrap your item in the newspaper directly; you don't want any newspaper ink to bleed onto your products.

In addition to packing paper, I also purchase **bubble wrap**. In my area, I have found Sam's Club to have the best price on bubble wrap. Bubble wrap is a MUST for protecting ceramics such as coffee mugs (of which I sell a lot of!). Again, after the item is wrapped securely in bubble wrap, I then use newspaper to further buffer it inside of the box.

Packing peanuts are always nice to have on hand to use in shipments, but buying them new is expensive. I save any that I get from online orders I myself place, and I let my friends and family know that I will gladly take their unwanted packing peanuts off of their hands. Most people are happy to get rid of the packing peanuts they have as they are a static mess to deal with and can't be recycled.

In order to close up your packages, you need **packing tape**. Clear packing tape can be found at the drugstores, big box retailers, office supply stores, warehouse clubs, and even the dollar stores. I purchase my packing tape at either Staples or Sam's Club. A case of Staples brand tape is $30 and lasts me a year; the 3M brand that Sam's Club sells contains six large rolls and lasts several months.

I also have a red **handheld tape dispenser** (sold right next to the tape). If you are just starting out, I recommend you buy a kit with the tape dispenser and some extra tape rolls. You can usually find such a kit for $10-15 in the tape section of most big box office and discount stores. You only need to buy the dispenser once and then tape refills as needed. Buy the best quality tape dispenser and tape you can as you will use less tape. Cheap tape isn't a good deal if you have to use more of it to seal up packages.

Shipping Station: Now that you have all of your shipping supplies, you need a place to prepare your shipments. If you have the space, it's nice to designate an area for shipping. I have a table in my office where my digital scale always sits at the ready. It's right next to my computer so that I can weigh items as I am listing them (again, lots more on this coming up). The most important thing is to have your digital scale on a flat surface so that you can get an accurate reading.

I have shelving for all of my boxes, envelopes, packing materials, and tape. Again, since I have an established business, I have a lot of materials. However, if you are just starting out, use an out-of-the-way space (perhaps in the basement) for your shipping supplies. You want to make sure your supplies (and the items you are selling) are away from any smoke, pets or other household odors. Yes, customers WILL complain if they find dog hair inside of their packages; and complaints about cigarette smoke can lead to negative feedback.

CHAPTER 5

WHAT ITEMS SHOULD YOU SELL ON EBAY

The most common question I get from people interested in selling on Ebay is, "What should I sell?" There is no easy answer to this because for every one item that does sell well on Ebay, ten more don't. There are hundreds of thousands of Ebay listings and millions of registered users. Learning what sells and what doesn't sell takes time and lots of trial and error. I have been selling on Ebay for nearly a decade, and I am still shocked at what sells for me. By the same token, I also pick up things I am sure will sell that don't.

The best place to find items to start selling on Ebay is your own home. In fact, when I first got started on Ebay in 2005, I started by selling unused items in my house. I quickly made $3,000 by selling my old work clothes (business casual attire I had accumulated from seven years of office work), books, CD's, DVD's, and house wares. These were all items I normally would have donated to Goodwill or sold for pennies on the dollar at a garage sale; but by taking a bit of extra time to list them on Ebay, I got a considerable amount of money for them.

Start gathering some items from around your home that you and your family are no longer using. Name brand clothing, designer handbags, toys, electronics, books, CD's, DVD's, kitchen gadgets, and collectibles can sell well online as long as they are in good, clean working condition. Being able to get $10 for a DVD on Ebay is a lot better than getting 50-cents for it at a garage sale!

In fact, if nothing else, you should look at selling on Ebay as a life skill. I firmly believe that schools should be teaching children the art of reselling, especially on a site like Ebay. Once you know how to sell on Ebay, you have the ability to generate quick cash for yourself, whether it's by selling your own items, sourcing products from thrift stores, or selling for other people.

If you are interested in finding products outside of your own home to sell, be sure to check out my books **101 Items to Sell on Ebay** and **101 MORE Items to Sell on Ebay**, both available on Amazon. But to get started, take a look around your house for the following items:

- CD's
- DVD's and Blu-Ray's
- Books
- Name-brand clothing and accessories
- Unused cosmetics
- Home décor from upscale stores such as Pottery Barn
- Tools
- Figurines
- Ceramics
- Dishes
- Flatware

- Anything licensed such as Disney or Peanuts

- Toys, both new and vintage

- Office supplies such as unopened printer ink and printer cartridges

- Craft supplies

These are just a handful of the categories of items that you can sell on Ebay. The longer you sell on the site, the more you'll discover about what things sell (and don't sell) online. Before you know it, you won't be able to browse in a store without wondering if you could sell their items on Ebay!

CHAPTER 6

WHAT'S WITH ALL OF THE FEES?

Ebay is sometimes jokingly called "FEEbay" by long time sellers. As a buyer, you aren't aware of fees because fees are all paid by the sellers. There are fees to list items, fees to relist items, fees when you sell items, and fees from using PayPal. Fees can take up to 25% (and sometimes more) of the sale price of an item!

However, 25% is much less than the 40-70% most consignment shops will charge you. Plus, since items sell on Ebay for much more than you could get from consigning them or selling them at a garage sale, you will still make more money by selling items on Ebay even after you pay the fees.

Why does Ebay charge fees? Well, they are a business! They have buildings to maintain and employees to pay, not to mention the sophisticated computer technology and servers required that allow people to buy and sell items on the site from all corners of the globe. Add in advertising costs, and you will realize that Ebay needs millions of dollars to run their site!

As far as PayPal, just as a retailer is charged a fee any time a customer swipes a credit card in their store, PayPal charges a fee whenever someone uses their services. Again, only sellers pay PayPal fees; and the fees for PayPal come out automatically whenever someone pays you. While your Ebay fees accumulate throughout the month, meaning you need to pay them either as you go or when you receive your monthly bill, PayPal fees are taken out of your account instantly with every payment you receive.

I will talk more about managing your Ebay fees later on in this book. However, just realize that part of selling on Ebay is paying their fees!

CHAPTER 7

THE FIRST STEPS

Whether you are looking to make selling on Ebay your job or just want to clear out some things from around your home, the first thing I tell all people to do is to BUY some things on Ebay before listing anything to sell. By becoming an Ebay BUYER, you will go through everything you need to do to set up both your Ebay and PayPal accounts, and you'll see how other sellers sell their items, which will go a long way towards teaching YOU how to sell yours.

If you have never bought anything on Ebay before, your first step will be to create an Ebay account as well as a PayPal account. Simply go to Ebay.com and they will prompt you to register.

When signing up for an account, you will first need to select a User Name, or Screen Name. Think carefully about the name you choose; you don't want to give out too much information (such as "singlewomanlivingalone") but you also don't want to have a crazy name no one understands (what does "dhioatg89yrew" mean?).

Since there are millions of registered Ebay users, chances are the first name you want to use may already be taken, so have a few options ready. If you think you might want to sell on Ebay consistently in the future, choose a name that reflects what you plan to sell. My Ebay user ID name is "AnnabellasGiftShop", which was my business name before

I even started selling on Ebay. My name tells buyers that I sell gift items, although I also sell vintage and secondhand things now, too.

Note that you will need to supply Ebay with your Social Security number and banking information, either a bank account or credit card. The Social Security number is for tax purposes; if you sell more than $20,000 a year on Ebay, they will send you a tax form to file. Now, since you picked up this book to simply learn how to sell on the site, you don't have to worry about paying taxes on the items you sell at first. However, you still need to give Ebay your Social Security number. Ebay's website is safe, so don't worry about providing them with your number; it's something all sellers must do.

You will also need to supply your banking information, which is done through PayPal. PayPal is Ebay's "bank"; it's the system they use for buyers to pay sellers and for sellers to pay their Ebay fees. While your PayPal account is in of itself a type of bank account, you will need to provide a source not only to withdraw money to but also as a backup to pay fees.

Here's a scenario to demonstrate why you need a back-up funding source: Let's say you sold 10 items on Ebay within a month. Every week, you went in and withdrew the funds in your PayPal account to your personal checking account, the account you have at your local bank. However, at the end of the month, Ebay sends you a bill for all of your seller fees.

Let's say those fees total $20 for all 10 items you sold. Since you have withdrawn all of your money from your PayPal account, you need a back-up funding source to pay those fees. So, to pay your fees, you issue payment to Ebay from your back up funding source. In this instance, let's say it is with your credit card.

When Ebay sends you notice that you owe your monthly fees, you have two options. One, you can initiate payment from your bank account or have it charged to your credit card. Or two, you can let the payment be made automatically. Ebay WILL get their money, so if you don't initiate payment, they will just take it from your bank account or credit card, whichever one you have set as your back up payment source. Note that if Ebay charges your fees to your credit card that you will need to then pay off your credit card, or else before long you will have accumulated a big balance of nothing more than fees!

I will talk more about fees and Ebay's monthly invoicing later in this guide (I know it seems overwhelming, but trust me, it's not!); but hopefully I've demonstrated Ebay's need for you to provide back-up funding sources.

I personally recommend having both your bank account AND a credit card on file with Ebay. The bank account is necessary for withdrawing your money (after all, you want to sell on Ebay to get money; and to get your money, you need to have somewhere to withdraw it to).

However, the credit card not only offers you the ability to charge any purchases you make or fees you might incur, but it also gives you a leg up on Ebay in terms of how many listings you can have. Ebay places limits on how many items new sellers can list at a time until you prove to them that you will pay your fees. By providing a credit card, Ebay is ensured of a way to get their money, and they will loosen up on your selling restrictions.

Ebay not only charges fees for listing items but also final value fees when items sell. However, these fees accumulate in your Ebay account, they aren't taken out automatically the way PayPal fees are. Therefore, every month Ebay wants the money you owe them. Having a credit card on file means that if you don't pay your fees from your PayPal or bank accounts that they can then charge the fees to your credit card.

I have my account set for my fees to automatically be charged to my card every month. However, I usually pay my fees as I go so that I don't have a bill at the end of the month. But sometimes I forget or am away, so the credit card ensures that Ebay gets their money and that my account remains in good standing.

So, once you have both your Ebay and PayPal accounts set up, it's time to do a little buying. There are millions of listings on Ebay's site, including lots of 99-cent items with free shipping (mostly little trinkets shipped from China). Look around and find some low-cost items to buy. The point of this isn't to get quality merchandise or to get things you really want, but to familiarize yourself with Ebay's buying system.

There are four kinds of sales on Ebay: Auction, Auction with Buy It Now, Buy It Now, and Buy It Now with Best Offer.

Auction items are items you bid on. Say you find an item you like that is listed at auction for 99-cents. In order to place a bid, you simply put in the minimum bid increment, which varies depending on the current bid. For 99-cent items, you can start bidding at 99-cents, and then you bid in 5-cent increments after that.

Auction with Buy It Now not only offers customers the chance to bid on items, but it also provides them the ability to buy the item outright without bidding. So, you may see an auction for 99-cents with a Buy It Now option of $3. You can either bid OR buy the item outright. Once the first bid is placed, the Buy It Now option disappears.

Fixed Price listings only offer the option of purchasing the item outright; there is no option to bid. While Ebay started as an auction site, more and more sellers now only offer their items at Fixed Price. When you click on the button to buy an item at Fixed Price, you are committing to purchasing it.

Fixed Price with Best Offer listings feature a set price from the seller but with the option of buyers submitting Best Offers for consideration. Let's say you see an item listed for $50 with the Best Offer option. You can submit an offer to the seller for $40. If they seller accepts, you are then required to purchase the item for $40. However, the seller could counteroffer, let's say coming back with a price of $45. You could accept the counteroffer, or you could make another counteroffer of your own. Or the seller could simply reject your offer outright. Most sellers accept reasonable offers.

If this if your first time buying on Ebay, try finding one of each of these types of listings to test each one out. Again, go for low price listings as your goal isn't to spend a lot of money but to gain experience in how the Ebay system works. You'll learn a lot about how YOU want to sell on Ebay by trying out each of the formats. Maybe you find that you love the negotiating that comes with the Best Offer option and decide to use that when you sell. Again, BUYING will help you with your own SELLING!

Buying items will teach you how to make payments through PayPal, which is super easy to do as PayPal is connected to your Ebay account. Once you commit to purchasing an item, you simply click through the link Ebay provides to submit payment via PayPal. It only takes a few clicks of your computer mouse to make your purchases!

Take note of the items as they are shipped to your door. Did they come within the time promised by the seller? How were things packaged? Did items come clean or were they dirty and smelly? Observing how other sellers' package and ship their items will go a long way towards teaching you the right and wrong way to ship YOUR items once you start selling!

Once you've actually purchased some items, you'll want to follow through with leaving **Feedback**. A unique feature of Ebay is their feedback system where both buyers and sellers can leave each other feedback on transactions. Buyers can leave sellers Positive, Neutral or Negative feedback; sellers can only leave buyers Positive feedback.

In addition to the Feedback rating, buyers and sellers can also leave comments. Buyers can also rate their experience using a five-star system on the following factors: **Item as Described**, **Communication**, **Shipping Time**, and **Shipping & Handling Charges**.

Good feedback is key to having a successful selling career on Ebay. Getting a negative feedback will seriously lower your overall feedback rating. A buyer who "dings" your stars (i.e. leaves you lower than the ideal 5-stars) hurts your seller rating.

A solid feedback score and seller rating not only make potential customers more likely to buy from you, but they are also important in maintaining your Ebay account. Ebay has cracked down in recent years, suspending accounts and getting bad sellers off of the site. You want to do everything that you can to make sure your buyer is happy; we'll go over this later on in this book.

As a buyer, you want to leave honest but fair feedback. If you get the item you ordered in the time the seller promised and it is in the condition it was advertised in, there is no need to leave anything other than 5-stars. Buyers who consistently leave negative feedback for most purchases are typically blocked by sellers. When it comes to feedback, I take the Golden Rule approach in that I leave the feedback for others that I'd want for them to leave me!

CHAPTER 8

MY EBAY

As an Ebay buyer and seller, you will be spending a lot of time on the **My Ebay** section of the site, which is your personal Ebay page. You will see the My Ebay link at the top of Ebay's homepage; I actually bookmark it so that I can hop onto it easily. You can also access some part of My Ebay through Ebay's mobile app, although it's important to realize that not all sections of the site are available through the app. While I can do some basic tasks on the app, I do the majority of my Ebay work on my desktop computer.

My Ebay is the hub of your Ebay activity. All of the items you are watching, bidding on, buying, or have purchased are listed here; as are any items you are selling, have sold, or have listed but ended without a sale. At the top of the page are tabs for Activity, Messages, Account, and Applications. On the left-hand side of the page is your Summary, under which are lots of different links to information about not only your account but Ebay in general.

Activity is the default page for My Ebay, where all of your buying and selling activities are located. You can change the look of this so-called "landing page" by clicking on the **Change** link on the right-hand side of the page. I have mine set to the **All Selling** setting. I have then further rearranged the blocks of activity on my page by using the little up and down arrows located on the right-hand side. While **Your Performance** is at the top and can't be moved, under that I have put

Sold, followed by **Active Selling**. While I have **Unsold** at the bottom, I actually always access this in the left-hand column of My Ebay (it is under Summary and then under Sell).

Take some time to explore everything on your My Ebay page under the Activity tab. Ebay frequently moves things around, adding some features and taking some away, so I won't walk you through every link in this book. But do click through and look around to familiarize yourself with all of the features available. Don't be afraid to change things as you can always undo them later.

The **Messages** tab brings up your Ebay messaging system. This is where you will find all communications from customers as well as any messages Ebay sends out to you. Don't worry about missing a message; a number will appear right on the Messages tab letting you know when new messages are there for you. Remember that all legitimate messages from Ebay and PayPal will be here; if you get a suspicious message from Ebay in your email inbox, you'll know it is a fake if a copy is NOT in your Messages folder.

The **Account** tab gives you a running total of your fees as well as what payment method you have on file, which you can change at any time. I have a credit card on file with Ebay so that any fees I owe are charged to that. However, I frequently go in and click on the **One-Time Payment** link to pay my fees as so that I don't end up with a huge bill at the end of the month.

On the left-hand side of the page under **My Ebay Views** is **My Account**, under which are a number of links to various aspects of your Ebay buying and selling preferences. Again, take time to click on each link to learn more about each. Make sure all of your information is correct, including your mailing address and email. Each link has even more links under it to explore. While it may seem tedious, take the time to look around and change the settings as you want them to be. Again, nothing is set in stone; if you change your mind later on, there isn't anything that you can't change.

The final tab is **Applications**, which is a new link for all of the various apps and programs available to assist you in your Ebay business. As a new seller, don't overwhelm yourself with this page. If you decide to make selling on Ebay a bigger part of your life, you can always check it out later on when your skills are more advanced. To be honest, the only app I use is the Ebay app on my iPhone!

CHAPTER 9

THE FIRST ITEMS YOU PLAN TO SELL

Once you've gotten comfortable using the Ebay site as a buyer, it's time to start selling! While it's tempting to quickly throw up a bunch of listings at once, I urge you to take it slow and start with just a few. Again, Ebay is a unique site with its own rules for buying and selling. It's easy to make mistakes (I've been on the site since 2005 and I still mess up now and then!), so it's important to take your time to get your listings right.

The first items you list should be like the first items you bought: low priced things that you are looking to gain experience from rather than making big money. The goal is to learn how to properly list items and ship them, not profit big right out of the gate.

Why not start off on Ebay selling a big-ticket item? New sellers are notorious for making mistakes and for experienced buyers taking advantage of them. It's easy for a new seller to have an error in their listing or in their shipping. Save your higher priced items for a bit further down the road when you are completely comfortable selling on Ebay. Trust me, it won't take too long for you to get there!

If you are simply looking to Ebay to sell some items from around your home, you likely already have some things in mind or maybe even a pile of stuff you want to list. Pick out five things that you are comfortable selling for less than $5. Maybe some CD's, a book, and a piece of clothing. Remember, the first items you sell are for EXPERIENCE, not profit.

Once you have five items, research them on Ebay's site to see what the current going price is. Ebay has an in-depth search tool that lets you narrow down items by all kinds of factors, including completed listings. To this day, I research every single item before I list it on the site. Sometimes an item is going for much more than I thought; other times, I find it isn't selling at all. Doing a bit of research will save you time and listing fees by realizing that you may be better off just donating your items or selling them at a garage sale as opposed to taking the time to list them on Ebay.

To look up the completed listings on your items, simply go to the Ebay website and type in the name of your item into the search bar at the top of the page. If it's a common item, there will likely be thousands of active listings on the site. However, it's not the active listings you want to look at. What sellers are ASKING for an item doesn't matter; what matters is what customers have actually PAID for the item.

Once the results for the active listings have come up, you need to narrow down your search. On the left-hand side of the screen is a column of search criteria. Scroll down until you see **Show Only**. Under that will be a few options, including **Completed Listings**. Click on Completed Listings, and the search will reset, showing the most recent listings that have ended with either a sale or no sale.

For the items that have sold, their prices will appear in green. You can further narrow down the search to only show you sold items by clicking on the **Sold Listings** on the left.

Browsing the completed listings will help you narrow down a price for your item. Sometimes items all sell for a similar price, making it easy for you to decide how to price yours. However, often the prices vary greatly. When this happens, you need to take a good look at your item and how it compares to the ones that have sold.

For instance, perhaps you have a designer pair of jeans that you only wore once. They are in excellent condition, just like the ones that have gotten top dollar recently on Ebay. However, there are lots of other pairs on the site that have sold for much less. Either the condition was poor or the seller made an error in pricing.

I see both happen a lot. Often, new Ebay sellers overestimate what their item is worth and ask too high of a price, resulting in no sale. Or a seller greatly underestimates the price and sells the item for too low. Usually when this happens, the seller started the item at auction for a low price and didn't attract many bidders. A bidding war can only happen when two or more people want an item. If you put up an item for 99-cents and only one person bids, all you will get for it is 99-cents.

The days of bidding wars on Ebay are mostly long gone. When I first started selling, I could put up anything and have multiple bidders on it within minutes. However, today there are hundreds of thousands of sellers with millions of products flooding the site. Even a popular, in-demand item usually has numerous listings, making it hard to get top dollar with auctions.

I only use auctions if I have absolutely no idea what an item is worth, or if an item has been sitting around a while and I want to get it sold. I rarely start out auctions for less than $9.99. When you do an auction, start it at the price you will be happy with getting. If you start an auction at only 99-cents for, don't be surprised when that is all it goes for.

CHAPTER 10

PHOTOGRAPHING YOUR ITEMS

Before you can list your items for sale on Ebay, you need to photograph them. Having good, clear photos of your items is essential in not only attracting customers but in getting top dollar.

I used to use a digital camera that I'd had for nearly 10 years to take all of my Ebay pictures, but for the past several years I've exclusively used my iPhone for photos. Today's smart phones are just as good, if not better, than many digital cameras; and taking pictures on your phone means you can upload them directly to Ebay through their app. Whether you use a digital camera or smart phone, the most important thing is that the pictures are clear, not blurry; that they are well lit and show the true color of the item; and that photos are cropped so that there isn't a bunch of white space around them. You want the item itself to be front and center.

A common mistake I see new sellers make is taking photos of their items on the floor or on a crowded counter. You don't want any other part of your home showing in the photo, just the item. Would you want to buy something that you know has been on someone else's floor or near their dirty sink?

An easy, cheap photo background is to take two pieces of foam board (I buy mine at Dollar Tree for $1 each) and place them together at a 90-degree angle (one laying on the table and then one propped up against the wall). This gives you a clean white background both under and behind the photo. I have used this system for nearly a decade, and actually have a video of it on my YouTube channel (along with lots of other Ebay videos); the link to my channel is at the back of this book. If you are selling clothing, hang the garment up on the back of a door. A white door is preferable, but if you don't have one, a wood door will do. Make sure all of the wrinkles are ironed out, the buttons all buttoned, and that the piece is lying flat against the door. If you decide you want to become a full-time Ebay clothing seller, you can invest in a mannequin; but to start out, the door method is just fine.

Whatever the item is that you are photographing, you'll want to take a lot of pictures of it from all angles. When people go into a brick-and-mortar store, they touch the items and turn them over in their hands. You want to give your Ebay customers the same feeling when they are looking at your listings. When I photograph a coffee mug, for instance, I take a picture of each of the four sides as well as from the top looking down into the mug and of the bottom.

Often when looking at multiple completed listings of items that have ended, the number one difference between ones that have sold and ones that haven't is the photos. Great photos go a long way towards selling items on Ebay, so take the time to get yours right!

CHAPTER 11

CREATING YOUR FIRST LISTING

So, you have your Ebay and PayPal accounts set up. You've purchased a few things on Ebay and left feedback; and hopefully you've gotten some feedback left for you as a buyer. You've chosen a few things to list, and you've taken pictures of those items. Now it's time to create your first listing!

While there are programs you can use to create your listings off-line, I still prefer to create my listings live on the Ebay site. Unless you have a full-scale Ebay business where you are listing thousands of items, listing things one by one on the site is actually easier, especially for those just starting out.

The first Ebay listing you create is the most labor intensive one as you will have to fill out all of the various fields, including all of the shipping options. However, once you have created your first listing, the second listing and all those that follow will be much easier as you can select the "Sell Similar" option, which will copy the information from the first listing into the second, meaning you'll only have to change certain fields, not start completely from scratch. We'll discuss that more after we walk you through creating your first listing.

Log into your Ebay account, and click on the **Sell** tab at the very top of the page on the left-hand side. Even if you've already been on the site earlier, you usually will have to log in again; don't worry, this is just an added level of Ebay security so that they are assured that it is indeed you logging into your account. Ebay has a lot of protections built into their site, so get used to have to re-log into your account frequently

Ebay offers an on-screen guided tour when you click on the Sell tab. Definitely follow along with this tutorial as it walks you through the selling process and all of the features in your My Ebay screen, which is the hub of your Ebay account. As we discussed earlier, all of your buying and selling activity is located in your My Ebay section.

When you are finished with the tutorial, click again on the Sell tab at the top of page. On the left-hand side is a column with **Selling Manager** in bold. Click on the link for **Drafts**.

After clicking on Drafts, the page will change and you will see a blue button that says **Create Listing**. Click on this, and then click on **Single Listing** to get started.

The first field to pop up is for the **Title**. A great title is key to selling your item as it will be what helps buyers find your listing. You want to use all of the character space allowed, even if it doesn't read as a proper sentence or headline. "Red Men's Shirt" is a bad title as it will be drowned out in the search against all of the other red shirts listed. However, "XL Red Mens Tommy Hilfiger Button Down Shirt Long Sleeve Cotton Extra Large" not only tells the customer exactly what the item is, but it is loaded with keywords to make finding the listing in the search much easier. There's no need to check the box to make your title bold or to enter a subtitle; these are just added features for which Ebay charges you extra fees. In all of my years of selling on Ebay, I've never once paid for these options.

After filling in the title area, you will need to select a **Category** for your item, which is another way a buyer will be able to narrow down their search. Let's stick with the Tommy Hilfiger shirt. Obviously, since this is a piece of clothing, you'll want to select the "Clothing, Shoes & Accessories" category. You'll then be able to narrow down the category even further by selecting "Men's Clothing" and then "Casual Shirts". Ebay gives you the option of selecting a second category for an extra charge, but one category is plenty.

If you have an Ebay Store subscription, you'll also be able to choose your **Store categories,** which you can set up when you create your Ebay store. Note that some sellers do not having any store categories, while others break their items down into very specific sections. To set up store categories, click on the **Marketing** tab at the top of your My Ebay page and select **Store**. Then click on the **Manage My Store** icon in the top right-hand corner of your store's front page. Under the **Store Management** section on the left-hand side, select **Store Categories** under **Store Design** to access the **Manage Store Categories** section.

Once you've chosen your Ebay category and store categories (if applicable), **Condition** is the next field you'll encounter. Representing the correct condition of your item is very important as buyers can file a claim with Ebay and get their money back if you say an item is new but is actually used, or if it is in worse condition that you state. Legally, once you take an item out of a store, it is used; so even if it still has the tags and has never been worn, it is technically used. However, new in box or new with tag items are almost always listed as "new" by Ebay sellers.

Depending on the category, there may be more choices than just new or used. In the clothing category, for instance, there are four: New with Tags, New without Tags, New with Defects, and Pre-Owned. If that Tommy Hilfiger shirt has been washed but never worn, it is still pre-owned.

There is also a **Condition description** field for you to write in any specific information you want the customer to know about. Be sure to disclose even the tiniest of issues. Flawed items can still sell, but you want to make sure detail any and all stains, rips, or cracks an item may have

One of the best pieces of advice I ever got for selling on Ebay was to under promise and over deliver. I often understate the condition of my items. If an item is in like-new condition, I say it's in great condition. If it is in good condition, I will say it is fair. Not only is condition highly debatable among buyers, but when a customer gets something in better shape than they thought it would be, they are always pleased. My feedback reflects this as a number of my customers write, "Better condition than expected!"

The next step in the listing process is to upload the **Photos** of your item. Ebay allows up to 12 pictures; take advantage of that by uploading lots of photos. As we discussed earlier, good, clear pictures will help sell your item for top dollar.

I actually upload my photos from my phone directly to Ebay and I do this in one of two ways. The first way is to skip inserting the pictures while creating the listing on my computer, saving the listing as a draft, switching to the Ebay app on my phone, opening the draft, and uploading the photos. Or I have a second way where I create a draft first on my phone by clicking on the Sell Similar option on one of my active listings. When I do this, a new listing is created. I delete the photos, add in the new pictures, and save the listing as a draft. I then switch back to my computer to complete the listing. I know this probably sounds very involved and complicated; but trust me when I say that once you've done this process a few times, it takes less than 30 seconds to complete going forward.

Back to creating your listing!

Next comes the **Item Specifics** fields. Again, depending on what category you are listing in, there could be a lot or only a couple of options. Only the fields with green stars next to them are mandatory; in the clothing category, up to nine categories can pop up, but you only need to fill out three. However, if you have the information the field is asking for, fill it in. Again, the more information you provide, the easier it will be for customers to find your item in the search results.

UPDATE: In late 2019, Ebay rolled out a vastly expanded Item Specifics section that has more fields to be filled out. Only those labeled as "Required" must be completed; but it is in your best interest to fill out as many as possible as doing so will aid your item being found in search.

The next section to fill out is **Item description**, which is where you really get to "sell" your item. Put in as much information as you can think of; the more details you give, the more likely you are to sell your item, plus it will drastically cut down on questions from potential buyers.

When listing a book, for instance, I type in everything that is on the cover page, including the publishing house. I also measure the book. You would not believe how many questions I get when I don't put in the measurements!

While all of these details may seem like a waste of time for you, remember that you are competing with thousands of others listings, especially if you are selling a popular item such as a current toy or video game. Let your buyers know the REAL condition of the item; and if it comes from a smoke-free home, mention that, too.

You can dress up your item description section with fonts and colors, but I prefer to keep it simple. Remember that buyers from all over the world will be looking at your listing, and they'll be using all sorts of devices (computers, smart phones, tablets) to access Ebay; which means crazy fonts can end up looking really messed up. I stick to Ariel or Times New Roman at a 12- or 14-point size and I stick to the color black. More and more, Ebay buyers are shopping on their mobile devices, so keeping your listing details simple will help your item screen to load cleanly onto customer's cell phones.

Once you've filled out the item description section, it's time for **Selling details**, which is where you will decide the **Format**, whether or not to list your list at Auction-style OR Fixed Price. This is where research comes into play. If you have done a completed listing search on an item and found out it has been selling at a consistent price, then set yours the same at Fixed Price. If prices are all over the place, price yours somewhere in the middle. Or you can take a risk and start an auction.

While Ebay used to be known solely for auctions, these days most experienced sellers list their items at Fixed Price. Most buyers who shop on Ebay now expect items to be at Fixed Price, so auctions tend to get overlooked.

I only put my items up for auction if I can't find any completed listings for them and have no idea what to price them as; or if I am looking to move inventory and decide to try auctions to move some things out and to generate traffic to my other listings. Mostly, though, I stick to Fixed Price listings so that I can set the price I want.

As a new seller, I would try a few items at auction starting at 99-cents for 7-days, just so you can get the experience of running an auction. However, for the most part, I would suggest you list your items at Fixed Price. As I said earlier, that gives people plenty of time to find your listing and hopefully buy your item.

Next up is **Duration**. If you are running an auction, you'll choose 1, 3, 5, 7, or 10 days. I personally prefer seven days, as it gives buyers a full week to find your listing. If you choose to list an item at Fixed Price, the only duration option is now Good 'Til Cancelled, which means your item will automatically be relisted every 30 days until it sells or is manually ended.

As I said, I usually run auctions for seven days as it gives people a full week to find the listing and bid. However, if I have a really hot item, I will run it for as few as 3 days knowing it will sell quickly.

Note that there is an option to schedule your listing to go live at a certain start time. While some experienced sellers do choose to pay for the option of scheduling their listings, most, including me, simply check the **Start my listing when I submit them** box.

In the **Price** field, you'll either enter in your starting bid price or your fixed price. If you do decide to run an auction, you will notice that you have the option to offer a Buy It Now price. This means that while you have a starting auction price, you also set a Buy It Now Fixed Price that buyers who don't want to bid can take advantage of. So, if you start an auction at 99-cents, you could also offer a Buy It Now price of $9.99. Note that extra fees apply if you offer a Buy It Now price on an auction listing. Also, if someone places a bid, the Buy It Now option will disappear and all buyers will now have to bid on the item; no one can buy it outright. Because of the fees, you should only offer the Buy It Now option on Auctions that you start out at a higher price.

For an additional fee, you can also set a *Reserve price* that the winning buyer will have to meet. I prefer to just start my auctions at the lowest price I'll be happy with rather than pay additional fees for offers or reserves.

The **Best Offer** feature can be added to both Auction and Fixed Price listings. You can also set up automatic accept and decline amounts. However, it can be advantageous to let all offers, even insultingly low ones, through as it keeps your store listings active in Ebay's algorithm. Ebay likes to see that customers are engaging with your listings, which helps your items get bumped up in search.

Quantity is simply the number of items you have for sale. If you are only selling one book, for instance, you just type in a "1". If you are selling multiple, identical copies of the same item – for instance, you have three copies of a video game – then you would type in the number of items you have. Note that multiple items must all be IDENTICAL, not only in that they are all exactly the same item but that the conditions are all the same, too. If you have two of the same shirts, one brand new with the tags and one that has been washed and worn, you will need to create two separate listings.

A **Private listing** allows your buyer's Ebay user names to be hidden; and the **Make a donation** option lets you donate a portion of your sales to the charity of your choice.

Under the **Payment options** section you will need to enter the email address of your PayPal account. As I talked about earlier, when a buyer pays you, the money will be transferred directly into your PayPal account. If you are offering an item at Fixed Price, you can require that the buyer pay immediately by selecting the **Require Immediate Payment When Buyer Uses Buy It Now**. This will prevent people from clicking on the item but then not paying for it. All of my Fixed Price listings require Immediate Payment.

As I mentioned earlier, Ebay is slowly implementing their own Managed Payments system. If you have opted in or been automatically enrolled, Ebay will walk you through the steps to set up your payment account.

In late 2019, Ebay began collecting **Sales tax** for the state's that required it. I used to have to collect sales tax on all orders within my state and submit a quarterly payment; however, Ebay now takes care of this for all sellers. Since the sales tax field is still in the listing templates, I still check the box even though I no longer have to collect the tax myself.

Finally, you can set up your **Return options**. I currently do not accept returns, so I leave both the boxes for Domestic returns and International returns unchecked. However, if you do decide to accept returns, you can choose whether the buyer has 14, 30 or 60 days to contact you; and you can decide whether you or the buyer will pay the return postage. In recent years, Ebay has heavily pressured sellers to offer "free returns", meaning sellers PAY the return postage. However, most sellers, including me, can't afford to absorb the cost of returns.

Whether or not you choose to accept returns, and whether or not you choose to make them "free" is only a decision you can make.

Now for the most confusing part of selling on Ebay for new sellers: **Shipping**!

There are dozens of carriers and ways you can ship packages. While UPS and FedEx are viable shipping options, when you are just starting out you will want to stick with shipping your packages through the United States Postal Service (USPS). The USPS provides the best value and service for small sellers, and Ebay has partnered with them to make shipping easy and cost-effective. Since the USPS is Ebay's preferred shipping partner, if you sell on Ebay, you will be using them a lot.

While there are dozens of ways you can ship a package through the Post Office, most Ebay sellers ship via one of four methods: Media Mail, First Class, Parcel Select, and Priority Mail. These four options are all for packages being shipped within the United States.

Media Mail is for, surprise, MEDIA! It is preferable to send books via Media Mail because they are heavy and you get a discounted rate. However, the low price also means that Media Mail is extremely slow, sometimes taking up to one month (although the Post Office claims delivery is 2-8 business days).

The following items qualify to be shipped via Media Mail: Books of at least eight printed pages; 16-millimeter or narrower width films and catalogs of films 24 pages or more; Printed music; Educational testing materials and printed educational materials; Sound recordings;

Playscripts and manuscripts; Loose-leaf pages and their binders of education medical information; and Computer-readable media.

Media Mail can NOT be used for advertising, video games, computer drives, or digital drives. The maximum weight for a Media Mail package is 70-pounds.

Some sellers try to cheat the system by shipping heavy, non-media items via Media Mail. This is a violation of USPS policy and can result in you losing your postal account. Post offices are notorious for opening Media Mail boxes to make sure they only contain approved media items, so be careful to follow the rules.

Media Mail items can only be shipped in plain boxes or envelopes, not in the Priority Mail boxes. When you print a label via Ebay (more on how to do this coming up), it will clearly state on the label which service you paid for. So, if you print a Media Mail label, it will say "MEDIA MAIL" at the top.

First Class: First Class MAIL is the service you use when you send a letter. One stamp equals one ounce; and you can mail a LETTER up to 3-ounces via First Class. However, First Class can also be applied to PACKAGES that are 4-ounces or higher, just at a higher rate than a letter. In other words, you can't just slap stamps on packages and send them off. Any package that weighs between 4-ounces and 16-ounces is eligible for First Class package shipping. While First Class packages ship for more than First Class Mail, First Class is much cheaper than Parcel or Priority. Just like Media Mail, First Class packages must be in plain boxes or envelopes; you cannot use the free Priority Mail boxes or envelopes to ship First Class packages.

Shipping items via First Class is where having a postal scale really comes in handy as you can get your package down to the exact ounce. Every ounce means more money spent, so it's important to get as close of a weight on your item as possible (I'll talk more about weighing your packages coming up). If you are using calculated shipping and having your customers pay the shipping charge, being able to offer them First Class Mail saves them money. If the package you are sending weighs 8-ounces, the difference between First Class and Parcel or Priority can be as much as $6.

However, even with a digital scale, finding the exact ounce can be hard as you need an item's weight before you list it. My trick, and one that I will talk more about later in this book, is to add 3-ounces to the weight of all items to account for packing materials. So, if you have a small item that will fit into a poly mailer that on its own weighs 5-ounces, list it as 8-ounces. That way when it is in an envelope with a sheet or two of packing paper, a packing slip and a label, you won't risk the Post Office sending it back for insufficient postage.

Parcel Select, formerly called Parcel Post, is for packages weighing over 16-ounces. Parcel is slower than Priority (shipping time can take up to two weeks, although the Post Office claims 2-9 business days), but it is cheaper for heavy shipments. Parcel shipments must be in plain boxes or envelopes; just as with Media Mail and First Class, you can't ship Parcel Select shipments in the Priority Mail boxes.

The cost of Parcel Select postage depends on the weight of the package and where it is going to. That is why it is smart to use Ebay's Calculated Shipping as the customer pays for the exact shipping for their zip code. The maximum weight for a Parcel package is 70 pounds.

While Parcel Select is a great option for heavy packages, you want to make sure to double check the cost between Parcel and Priority when you are creating your shipping label through Ebay (again, I will be going over how to do this coming up). Depending on how far away the package is going, Priority Mail may be the cheaper option.

As an example, I am in Iowa, centrally located from both coasts in the middle of the country. For packages weighing less than four pounds, it is often cheaper for me to ship via Priority Mail over Parcel Select. Plus, I get to use a Priority free box, and I get a discount on postage by shipping directly through Ebay.

What is great about shipping through Ebay is that you can look at all of the package and price options before paying for and printing a label. So, you can find the best rate for your shipment. It's always nice when a customer pays for Parcel but then you can upgrade them to Priority. Not only do you save money, but the item arrives much faster. Don't worry, I will be going over how to do this in later on in this book.

Of course, this brings up the issue of overcharging the buyer. Now, if a customer pays for Parcel but I am able to give him Priority for a dollar or two less, I don't worry about the difference. I know that the buyer will view Priority shipping as an upgrade on my part, which will result in great feedback for me. The bit of money I "make" from the difference will just go towards my packing supplies. However, if the difference is several dollars or more, I will refund the buyer the difference. Again, since everything goes through PayPal, issuing a partial refund is easy and will make the buyer very happy!

Priority Mail is for packages weighing over one pound that need to get to their location quickly, typically 2-3 business days. Note that "business days" means weekdays and doesn't include Saturdays and Sundays. If you ship an item out on a Friday, it may not be processed at the Post Office until Monday. From there, it will have an additional 2-3 days before it reaches the customer.

As I explained above when talking about Parcel Select, sometimes Priority Mail can be the cheaper option. For me, this is often true for packages weighing less than four pounds that are going as far as the East coast. I also get a shipping discount because I ship directly through Ebay, and I get the Priority Mail boxes for free. In fact, the vast majority of my shipments go via Priority Mail as nine times out of 10 it ends up being the cheapest option for packages between one and four pounds.

Priority Mail has other bonuses over Parcel Select including FREE tracking when you purchase the label online, Saturday delivery, and FREE Carrier Pickup. I utilize Carrier Pickup to have my mail carrier pick up my packages; in order to have her take my packages; however, I have to have at least one Priority Mail package. If I have all Parcel Select packages, for example, I can't request the free pickup. Since I work from home, Carrier Pickup is a blessing as I don't have to make multiple trips to the Post Office every week!

Of course, the best thing about Priority Mail is the FREE boxes! There are many sizes of Priority Mail boxes, including Regular, Flat Rate, and Regional options. The USPS website has a wide variety of box sizes to choose from, including starter sets where you can get a selection of sizes. Not only are the boxes FREE to order, buy your carrier will deliver them to your house for FREE, too!

While the Post Office promotes their Flat Rate boxes as the best price, for packages less than four pounds, Regular Priority Mail is usually cheaper. Why? When it comes to Priority Mail, it's not just the weight but also the distance a package has to travel.

As I mentioned previously, I live in Iowa. I can send a 2-pound package to Minnesota for a little more than $7. However, that same package costs over $10 to ship to California. If that package is going to New York, the postage is around $9. To Hawaii or Alaska, the cost jumps to $13. Again, it's not just the weight but the distance the package has to travel.

The type of Priority Mail box (Regular, Flat Rate or Regional) doesn't affect the speed of delivery. Priority is Priority. The difference in the shipping cost depends on the type and size of the box.

A **regular Priority Mail box** is priced by weight and the zip code to which it is being shipped. You can ship Priority Mail packages in regular boxes and envelopes, too, not only in the branded Priority boxes. The maximum weight for a Priority Mail package is 70 pounds. If using your own box, note that the maximum combined length and girth is 108-inches, which means the combined measurement of the longest side and the distance around the thickest part of the package can't be more than 108-inches.

A good rule of thumb for shipping packages via Priority Mail is that they can be no larger than 12x12x12-inches. Any box over that size must ship via Parcel or through another shipping carrier such as UPS or FedEx. The Post Office also provides FREE Priority Mail stickers to put on plain boxes and envelopes. I keep a roll of the stickers on hand for when we ship Priority packages in plain boxes.

Flat Rate Priority Mail boxes have a set price. You can pack them up to 70-pounds and pay one flat rate no matter where the package is going. However, there are various sizes of Flat Rate boxes and envelopes, each with its own price. The Post Office is constantly raising prices; but as of this writing, the envelopes and small boxes start at $7.35, the medium boxes ship for a bit over $14, and the large box are close to $20. The price varies depending on whether you print the labels yourself (cheaper) or have the Post Office print them (more expensive).

While the Post Office heavily promotes Flat Rate boxes as the best option, Flat Rate is often times more expensive than shipping via regular Priority. For instance, say you have a ceramic dish that weighs four pounds once it is in a shipping box. If you put it in a Medium

Flat Rate box, it will cost over $14 to ship anywhere in the country. Now, if you are in Florida and your buyer is in California that works out to be a great deal. However, if your buyer lives in your state or in a surrounding one, you'll pay much less in shipping by choosing regular Priority.

Again, by using Ebay's shipping tool, you will be able to see and compare all of the options available so that you can find the best deal (and I will show you how to do this coming up). However, note that if a customer pays for Priority, you need to ship the item Priority. Priority is an Expedited Service and is the fastest option as compared to Media, First Class or Parcel. So, if your buyer pays for Priority and you downgrade them to Parcel, they are rightfully going to be angry.

Regional Rate Priority Mail boxes are a new offering from the Post Office. There are four different sizes available: A1, A2, B1, and B2. I have found that the A1 and A2 boxes are often cheaper than the Regular Priority Mail boxes for the shipments I do. For instance, I can ship a lot of heavy silverware in a Regional Rate box and pay $9 versus over $14 for the Medium Flat Rate box.

The downsides to Regional Rate are that the boxes themselves are on the smaller size and they have lower weight limits (15 pounds for the A and 20 pounds for the B boxes. However, I keep a supply on hand in case I find that they are the best option. Again, since I ship via Ebay, I can look at all of the shipping options before purchasing a label.

International shipping used to be such a huge headache that most sellers avoided it altogether. While you certainly don't need to ship to Canada, South America or overseas, doing so will greatly increase your business. Fortunately, Ebay now offers their **Global Shipping Program**, an optional program you can opt into. Truth be told, Ebay will most likely put you in it whether you want to or not. I specifically opted OUT of the program twice, only to be put back in it. So now I am enrolled, and it has been smooth sailing ever since.

When a seller offers international shipping and opts into the Global Shipping Program, packages are sent to a sorting facility here in the United States. When I get an international shipment notification through Global Shipping, the label that prints out and the postage paid is to a facility in Kentucky. After the package arrives at the facility, Ebay takes full responsibility for it, including filling out customs forms and putting on the postage to send to the country of the buyer. Once a package reaches the Ebay facility, Ebay takes full responsibility for it; meaning if it is lost or if it arrives damaged, Ebay, not the seller, is responsible.

Because international shipping is now so easy using Ebay's Global Shipping program, there really is no reason not to opt into it. Opening up your sales to international customers will greatly increase your sales, and now printing a label is as easy at printing one for the United

So, now that you understand the basic four categories of USPS shipping options, it's time to choose the ones you want to offer for your listing. One of the biggest mistakes new Ebay sellers make it trying to guess at shipping costs, which results in them either overcharging customers or undercharging them and losing money on shipping. However, using **Calculated Shipping** will protect you and your customers from incorrect postage costs.

I am a firm believer in using Calculated Shipping on Ebay. If you have a digital scale, there is no reason not to. Calculated Shipping means the buyer pays the exact shipping cost for the weight of the item and for the zip code it is being shipped to.

While more seasoned Ebay sellers like to experiment with "free" shipping (i.e. building the cost of shipping into the price of an item), when you are just starting out, I recommend you stick to Calculated Shipping and have the buyer pay shipping. This will protect you from LOSING money by trying to guess shipping costs. It also ensures a fair shipping rate for the customer, which will in turn mean you won't get angry customers who figure they were overcharged for shipping. You can experiment with free shipping once you are more comfortable selling and shipping.

So, you have a digital scale and are ready to create a listing using Calculated Shipping. It's so easy to do; here's how:

First, put your item into the box you will likely ship it out in. Note that the box doesn't have to be the exact one you will end up shipping the item in; you just want a box close to the size and weight of one you will be using. Boxes can easily add up to one pound of weight to a shipment, so you definitely need to get an idea of what box you will be using.

If you are selling a coffee mug, for example, place it in a 7x7x6-inch Priority Mail box or a similar sized box. Set the box on the digital scale and note the weight. Perhaps it comes out to 1-pound and 4-ounces.

So, in the Ebay listing under package weight, you put in 1-pound and 4-ounces, right? WRONG! When you are dealing with weights above 4-ounces (remember, 16-ounces or less can go via First Class Mail; and since the mug is not a book, it can't go via Media Mail), you do NOT need to know the EXACT weight; you only need to know the RANGE between pounds. Understanding that you only need to know the RANGE will make your shipping process go much more smoothly.

If a mug in a box weighs 1-pound and 4-ounces, you simply select the 1-2-pound range under Calculated Shipping. You do NOT need the exact ounces. In fact, because the box will actually weigh MORE than 1-pound 4-ounces when it ships out (due to packing materials) that initial weight won't be accurate, anyway.

See how easy it actually is when you only need to know the weight RANGE? 1-2 pounds, 2-3 pounds, 3-4 pounds, etc. When an item is being shipped via Parcel Select, Priority Mail, or Media Mail, you only need to know the RANGE of weight. There is no need to worry about being exact down to the ounce!

I mentally add 3-ounces to all packages to account for packing materials. Yes, packing paper, newspaper, bubble wrap, packing peanuts, enclosures, and tape will all add additional weight to the shipment. So, for the mug in the box that weighs in at 1-pound and 4-ounces, I note the weight as being 1-pound and 7-ounces. However, I still don't need to put in that exact weight. I only need to put in that it is 1-2 pounds.

Mentally adding in the packaging material weight is necessary for when packages are close to going to the next pound. For instance, say you have an item in its shipping box with a beginning weight (before packing materials) of 1-pound and 15-ounces. Obviously when you add in packing materials, the weight is going to bump up to over 2-pounds and will need to be listed in the 2-3-pound range on Ebay. The same is true if the initial weight is, say, 2-pounds and 13-ounces. When you add in another 3-ounces for packing materials, the weight will be at 3-pounds and will need to be listed in the 3-4-pound range.

So, now that you understand about the shipping options and weights, let's set up the Shipping Details in an Ebay listing!

The shipping section within an Ebay listing is located about three quarters of the way down the page under **Shipping Details.** You will be selecting the shipping services first and adding the weight last.

The first section is for **Domestic Shipping.** The drop-down menu lets you choose from four options: "Flat: same cost to all buyers"; "Calculated: cost varies by buyer location"; "Freight: large items over 150 lbs."; and "No shipping: Local pickup only". You simply need to select the **Flat** OR **Calculated** options before moving on to the next step.

Once you have chosen Flat or Calculated, you will need to select **Services.** This is where your digital scale comes into play. If you have a lightweight item weighing under one pound (don't forget to add in the 3-ounces for packing material), then you will be able to choose "USPS First Class Package (2 to 5 business days)". However, you can also add in other options under that. I usually offer "USPS Priority Mail (1 to 3 business days)" for the second option. If you want to offer more than one shipping option, simply click on "Offer additional service".

The vast majority of my orders are over 1-pound, so I always offer "USPS Standard Post (2 to 9 business days)" as my first option since it is promoted as an "Economy Service" and gives the impression that it is the cheapest option available to the buyers. Note that "Standard Post" is actually "Parcel Select". I then offer "USPS Priority Mail (1 to 3 business days)" as the second option for buyers who want to choose an expedited shipping service.

As you will see when you look at all of the shipping options, there are a lot to choose from. I know that looking at all of the choices is very overwhelming for new sellers; but just remember to focus on the four I've talked about, which on Ebay are listed as "USPS Media Mail (2-8 business days)"; "USPS First Class Package (2 to 5 business days)"; "USPS Parcel Select (2 to 9 business days)", and "USPS Priority Mail (1 to 3 business days)". While you may select other options such as Flat

Rate or Regional when you actually go to print a label (more on this in the next section), you only need to offer your buyers any one of those options in the actual Ebay listing.

The next choice you need to make is your **Handling time,** which is the number of days it will take you to ship the item after receiving cleared payment. As Ebay points out, buyers like to get their items fast, so you'll want to choose a handling time between 1 and 3 days.

Because I work from home and utilize Carrier Pickup, I offer a handling time of "2 business days". This means that I ship my items with two BUSINESS DAYS (i.e. weekday) after a buyer's payment clears. If a buyer pays for their item on a Tuesday, I will ship it out on Wednesday or Thursday. However, if they don't pay until Friday, their item won't ship until Monday.

The next field is **Handling cost.** I made the decision years ago to NOT charge a handling fee. Ebay is an extremely competitive marketplace with millions of people buying and selling. You need to make your prices as attractive as possible, and a handling fee will only make your items more expensive. Since I use Calculated Shipping and get discounts for printing my labels through Ebay, I consider the small amount I save on shipping to be my handling fee. The extra money goes towards buying packing paper, bubble wrap, boxes, and tape.

Next up is **Combined shipping discounts.** If you have a lot of items to sell and think that people will be buying multiples from you, you can select the "Combined Shipping Discounts" option and set up

"Combined payments", "Flat shipping rule", and "Calculated shipping rule".

The "Combined payments" option allows buyers to send you one payment for multiple items purchased. If you have hundreds of CD's listed, for instance, a buyer who purchases three would be able to pay for all of them in one transaction.

The "Flat shipping rule" allows customers to pay shipping on the first item and then pay a flat fee for each additional item. So, if they buy three CD's, they would pay the full shipping on one, and an additional amount set by you (say, $1) for each of the other two.

The "Calculated shipping rule" allows you to specify whether you want multiple items combined into a total weight for shipping or if you want to give a discount based on the combined weight.

To protect myself from customers clicking on items and then not paying for them, I actually check the "Require immediate payment when buyer uses Buy It Now" option under the "Select how you'll be paid" section. Since I sell a wide variety of items, it is rare than anyone purchases more than one thing at a time from me. However, under the "Combined payments" section, I do have the "Buyers can send one combined payment for all items purchased from me within 14 days" option selected. Note that the immediate payment required option only works on Fixed Price listings, not Auctions.

The next section is for **International shipping.** I recommend just going with **Ebay's Global Shipping Program**, which means you will simply ship any sold items to Ebay's shipping center in Kentucky. From there, they will take care of all customs forms and assume responsibility for shipping the package internationally. Since you will be shipping the item to Ebay's US processing center, the buyer will pay the shipping charges offered under the "Domestic services".

Finally, you are now at the **Package weight & dimensions**, where you will put in the weight of the package. First, Ebay has a **Package type** field where you can choose from four options: "Letter", "Large Envelope", "Package (or thick envelope)", or "Large Package". If you are selling small to mid-size items, you can simply select the **Package (or thick envelope)** option. That is the only option I ever choose.

Next is a field for the **Box dimensions.** Good news – you can completely skip this! The only time you would need to provide a box size up front is if you are shipping an unusually large item. You will need to add your box size when you go to print the item if it is shipping via Parcel or Priority. You never need to provide the box size for Media or First Class. Again, stick to boxes that are 12x12x12-inches or less and you'll be fine.

Last is the field to enter is **Weight.** If you are shipping something that weighs one pound or less, simply choose the first option, "1 lb. or less" and enter the ounces. Here's a tip: No matter how many ounces the package weighs, put in 16 ounces. Yes, it will result in slightly overcharging some packages; but just chalk up any additional funds to your handling fee. For items weighing a pound or more, simply select the range as I talked about earlier. 1-2 pounds, 2-3 pounds, 3-4 pounds, etc.

Finally, you can **Exclude shipping locations**. If you are shipping internationally on your own and not using Ebay's Global Shipping program, I strongly advise blocking buyers in certain areas of the world that are prone to fraud and missing packages. Known trouble spots are all of African and the Middle East as well as Italy. Most international buyers on Ebay are from Canada, the U.K. and Australia anyway, and those are all safe place to ship to. However, where to sell to is completely up to you. If you are nervous about shipping internationally at all, even though Global Shipping, stick to domestic shipments until you feel more confident.

The next step to completing your is to click on the **List item** button at the bottom of the page, which will make your listing live and for sale on Ebay's site. However, you can first **Preview** the listing to see what it will look like when live; and you can also **Save as draft** if you still need to add some details to it.

After I submit a listing, I like to open it up to review what it actually looks like on the site. Sometimes I am able to quickly catch a mistake I may have made in the title or on a photo. I also utilize the "share" buttons located within each live Ebay listing to share it out to Facebook, Twitter and Pinterest.

CHAPTER 12

YOUR SECOND LISTING

Once you've gotten one Ebay listing under your belt, the second one will be super easy as the first one created a template for all your future listings. Now when you are ready to create a new listing, you simply click on one that you've already done and then click on **Sell Similar.** What Sell Similar does is copy the information from that listing into a new listing. Then you only need to change the photos, item specifics and shipping weight for your new item. You don't have to recreate every single policy with every single new listing.

Let's say your first listing was for a book. You've created that listing and it is live on Ebay's website. Now you want to list a coat. You simply click on the listing for the book and then click on Sell Similar at the top left-hand corner of the listing. A new page will open that will look exactly like the book listing, but you can now edit it. Change the fields that will make the listing for the coat instead of the book: Title, Category, Condition, Photos (make sure you delete the old photos before uploading the new ones), Item Specifics, Item Description, Selling Details, and Shipping Details.

Perhaps you had the book listed at Auction with the buyer paying for calculated Media Mail shipping. For the coat, however, you want to list it at Fixed Price with Free Shipping. So, you'll need to change the selling format and the shipping options within the new listing.

However, you don't have worry about changing your return policy or excluded shipping locations as those carried over from the book listing.

Under Shipping Details, since you are doing calculated shipping and have set up those specifics in your first listing, you only need to change the weight of the item and how you will ship it. Since clothing cannot go Media Mail, and because the coat weighs over a pound, you will have to choose Parcel or Priority. I actually give my customers a choice: the lower cost Parcel and the more expensive Priority. The customer feels they are getting a deal with the free Parcel shipping option I'm offering in this instance, but they can also pay to upgrade to Priority if they want the coat faster.

As you did with the first listing, after you've changed all of the relative fields and added in the new photos, you simply hit the "List Item" icon. You can then open that listing, hit "Sell Similar" again, and start on your next listing.

The "Sell Similar" trick is so fast and easy; I can't remember the last time I actually created a new listing from scratch. Note that you can access the "Sell Similar" in a listing by either clicking on it or by viewing all of your listings on your My Ebay page. When looking at your My Ebay page, you will see a drop-down menu next to all of your listings. One of the choices there is "Sell Similar".

The listing process gets easier and faster with every new item you list. While it can be overwhelming at first, trust me that in no time you will be listing items like a pro!

CHAPTER 13

WHAT TO DO WHEN AN ITEM SELLS

Finally, the most exciting part of selling on Ebay has arrived: You've actually SOLD something! Now it's time to print your label and package up the order!

Ebay will notify you via email when you have made a sale, so be sure to check your email regularly when you have items listed. Note that these "your item has sold" emails are NOT copied to your Ebay messaging folder. However, when you log into Ebay and go to your My Ebay page, you will see the sold items listed there.

In My Ebay is your list of Sold items. Next to the items that have sold is a drop-down menu where you can find options such as Contact Buyer or Resolve a Problem. There is also a **Send an Invoice** option. Note that some buyers WANT you to send them an invoice after they buy an item, even though the shipping options are already set up for them. Fortunately, a quick click sends an invoice; so be prepared to do that occasionally.

I have my Fixed Price listings set so that buyers have to pay immediately. However, buyers obviously can't pay immediately when they are bidding on items through an Auction, so you'll likely have to send invoices to auction winners.

If you have chosen to sell internationally using Ebay's Global Shipping program, Ebay will handle the invoicing for you. So, if someone in the United Kingdom buys an item from you, you actually won't be able to invoice them. Ebay will do it on their end as they will be figuring out the shipping as the customer will pay you the cost to send the item to Ebay's Global Shipping center, and then they will also pay Ebay to ship that item overseas.

Remember that Ebay gives buyers four days to pay for their items, so don't hound customers who are slow to pay. If I don't receive payment immediately, I send an invoice. Then the day before payment is due, I send a "friendly" reminder that their PayPal payment is due by the following business day. If they don't pay by the next day, I open a case using the "Resolve a Problem" option.

Once a customer pays for their item, the default on the drop-down menu next to the item in My Ebay changes to **Print Shipping Label.** All you need to do is click on that link and you will be taken to Ebay's label printing screen. Please note that you may have to log in again due to Ebay's tight security settings.

The Ebay label printing screen has **Print your shipping label** at the top, along with a summary of the order. Listed will be what the buyer paid for the item and how much they paid for shipping (unless you offered free shipping, in which case that number will be 0). On the left-hand side will be the buyer's address as well as your address.

In the middle of the screen is the section called **Select package type.** Since you set up your shipping preferences when you created your listing, the United States Postal Service will be the default Carrier. Choose your Package type, Custom size if you are shipping using your own box or regular Priority Mail or Carrier packages if you are using a USPS Flat Rate box or envelope.

For Custom size, simply enter in the weight and size of the box. Again, if the package is over one pound, you don't have to enter ounces; if it weighs 1-pound and 8-ounces, you can simply enter 2-pounds and 0-ounces. If the package is under one pound, you will want to enter in the ounces to get the best First-Class rate available.

If you are using a USPS Priority Mail FLAT RATE box, select Carrier packages to choose which box or envelope you are using. You do not have to enter weight or dimension if you are shipping in a Flat Rate box or envelope, including Regional Rate boxes.

Next is the section **Select service.** Here is where you will choose which shipping service your package will be shipped through, which for most people is USPS. The service the buyer paid for (usually the first option you gave them) will be the default option. However, you can play around with the options to see if you can get a better rate.

Let's say you sold a book that has a shipping weight of 2-pounds. The buyer selected the Media Mail option, which was the first choice given to them. Since you already had 2-pounds as the weight in the listing, there is nothing more for you to do. The Carrier is the United States

Postal Service. The Shipping Service is Media Mail. The weight is 2-pounds. Since all the fields are correct, all you need to do is click on the blue "Purchase Postage" icon on the right. You will be directed to PayPal (again, you may need to log in) where you will confirm the purchase of the label. The money to pay for the postage will be taken out of your PayPal account and the label will print.

On the other hand, let's say you listed a coffee mug in the 1-2-pound range and Parcel Select was the default option. Change it to the Priority Mail option to see what the price on the screen changes to. Depending on where the buyer lives, the price could go up or down. Let's say it goes down to a lower rate. That means you can ship the mug in a free Priority Mail box, the buyer will get it faster than if it were going Parcel Select, and you will profit a small handling fee from the excess.

However, you may find that Parcel Select IS the best price, so you can just stick with that. When you ship online, you get FREE tracking with First Class, Parcel and Priority (Media Mail tracking has a small fee). You will also notice a discount on First Class and Priority shipping for printing the labels online. The free tracking and discount postage are two of the best reasons for shipping online!

Before printing the shipping label, you can also add in **Protection**, such as Require Signature or Added Insurance (I only choose these for items of significant value). You can also decide if you want to **Customize your label by** displaying the postage cost or adding custom text. I do NOT check this box, as I don't want the buyer to see what the postage actually cost. Even a difference of a few cents can upset some customers, so I find it is better to just leave the price off of the label.

I DO have the Send a message to the buyer field filled out so that the customer gets confirmation when their item has shipped along with the tracking number. Since I use "Sell Similar" when creating listings, this information remains pre-filled in all of my listings.

So, you've chosen your shipping service and double checked the weight. Everything is ready to go, so now all you have to do is click on the big blue **Purchase and print label** button. If your buyer paid for the item through PayPal, the money for the item AND for the postage will be in your PayPal account, minus a small fee for using PayPal. Remember that PayPal fees are taken out automatically. When you print the label, the money for the postage will be taken out of your account and paid directly to the United States Postal Service. Ebay and PayPal handle the entire transaction for you.

Note that if you offered "free shipping", the postage cost will also be taken out of your PayPal account. So, if you sell a shirt for $15, offer free shipping, and it costs $5 to ship, don't be surprised when your balance ends up being under $10 after you pay for postage and PayPal fees, which are deducted after each transaction. And remember that you still need to pay your Ebay fees on top of that; you can pay as you go along or wait for one big bill at the end of the month. I advise paying as you go; before I withdraw any money for myself, I first pay my Ebay fees so that they don't pile up on me.

After you print your label, you also have the option of printing a packing slip. Simply click on **Open packing slip** if you would like to print one. I always include a packing slip in my orders, but not all sellers do. Again, the decision is yours to make.

Once your label has printed, both you and the buyer will receive notice from Ebay that the package has shipped. The tracking information will be included in this notice, and it will also be uploaded onto the item transaction page for both you and your buyer to access on your respective My Ebay pages. This is a wonderful feature as you, your customer and Ebay now have confirmation from the USPS that the label has been printed. You don't have to manually type in tracking; and if there are any issues with a lost package, you'll be able to easily show that you indeed did ship the item.

CHAPTER 14

PACKAGING UP ORDERS

Now that you have your label printed, all that is left to do is to seal up your package and attach the label to it! Since you weighed the item in the box or envelop you planned to ship it in before you ever listed it, you'll now want to go ahead and start packaging the item.

Even when selling used item and using secondhand packing materials, it is still important to take time to package up your items in a clean and professional manner. I keep all sorts of packaging materials on hand, everything from recycled packing paper to bubble wrap. As you are just starting out, try and use items from shipments you have gotten. If you don't have anything around, ask friends and family for any boxes, bubble wrap and packing peanuts they may have.

If you are just going to sell on Ebay occasionally, you might be able to get most of your shipping supplies for free by reusing what you have or asking for people to give you their leftovers. However, it's important that whatever you use is CLEAN and from SMOKE-FREE HOMES! If you are a smoker, be sure to keep your inventory AND your packing supplies in an area away from the smoke. If your buyer detects even the slightest scent of cigarettes, they WILL complain!

Using a combination of packing paper, bubble wrap, and/or packing peanuts, carefully wrap the item and make sure it is surrounded by a buffer of packaging material in the box. I do use newspaper to create a barrier around the item and the box sides, but I always make sure the item itself is wrapped in paper or bubble wrap away from the newsprint to prevent any print from rubbing off on the item.

If you are printing your shipping labels onto actual labels, you'll just need to remove the backing and stick the label to the package. However, if you are printing your labels onto paper, you'll need to use clear packing tape to adhere the label to the outside of the box. It usually takes me three small pieces to cover the label and to make sure it is stuck on tightly. The only part of the label that I do NOT cover with tape is the bar code. You'll want to leave the bar code free of the tape so that it can be easily read by the Post Office's scanning equipment.

Once your label is affixed to your package, it is ready to be shipped out! If you are at home and can arrange for pickup, you'll definitely want to take advantage of the FREE Carrier Pickup service. As long as you have at least one Priority Mail package, your postal carrier will pick up all of your packages for free. You do need to request package pick up the night before, however.

If you aren't able to be home for Carrier Pickup and need to take your packages to the Post Office, note that you will likely have to stand in line and hand them to a clerk. If you end up shipping out a lot of packages and develop a good relationship with the clerks, they may allow you to simply leave your packages on the counter. If you do hand them directly to a clerk, they can scan them and give you a receipt. I usually skip this since I have the tracking information from Ebay loaded onto my account.

CHAPTER 15

COMMUNICATING WITH CUSTOMERS

It is against Ebay's policies for buyers and sellers to communicate off of the Ebay site regarding a transaction. All communication needs to be done through the Ebay messaging system. Not only does this provide an easy way for you to keep track of all messages from both Ebay and customers, but it protects you as a seller as there will be an online record of all communications. So, if you are ever harassed or threatened by a customer, you can easily report it to Ebay and they will handle it.

At the top of your My Ebay page is a tab for Messages. It is here that you will find all messages that are sent to you and where you can send messages yourself. You can modify your messaging settings under the Account tab at the top of your My Ebay page. I have mine set so that I receive an email message to my email inbox (on my computer) whenever I receive a message. I then know to log on to Ebay to reply to it.

It's important to keep communication with your buyers friendly and professional, and to not send messages to them needlessly. When a customer buys an item, Ebay automatically sends them a notice that they have committed to purchasing the product and they need to pay. There is no need for you to send them a message demanding payment. I have seen so many new Ebay sellers get into trouble doing this.

From time to time, someone will bid on an item at auction and not pay; or if you don't have Immediate Payment Required on your listings, someone may click on it but not pay. This is the nature of Ebay, so expect non-paying bidders to pop up now and again. If I have an item up for auction and it ends with a winning bidder, I log onto Ebay, go to My Ebay, and send them an invoice. If they haven't paid in three days, I send them a friendly note reminding them that their payment is due. If by day four they still haven't paid, I open a claim through Ebay and let Ebay handle it from there. Typically filing a claim results in the buyer paying; but if they don't, Ebay will close the case in your favor and you're recoup all fees associated with the listing. And then you can simply hit "Relist" to put the item up for sale again.

As a new seller, you may also have to deal with people praying on your inexperience by sending you messages trying to get you to sell them an item for less than you have listed. If you are open to accepting offers, you need to set up the Best Offer option in your listing; buyers should NOT contact you to request a discount or to ask you to sell things to them off of Ebay. To stay safe, keep all of your transactions ON Ebay and report anyone who is trying to get you to deal with them off line.

If anyone sends you a message with profanity, report them to Ebay. The same goes for any messages that threaten to leave you negative feedback if you don't do what they say. Don't respond to threats of any kind; just report the buyer to Ebay.

If a buyer hasn't caused you any trouble, you'll want to leave them positive feedback as soon as they have paid for their item and you have shipped it. Some sellers will tell you to withhold feedback until a customer leaves it for you, but I don't agree with this. If a customer has paid for their item and you haven't had any issues with them, they have fulfilled their part of the transaction and deserve positive feedback. Since Ebay no longer allows sellers to leave negative feedback for buyers, your only choices are to leave positive feedback or no feedback at all. I always type something like, "Thank you for your order and immediate payment!" in the feedback description.

As a new seller, getting feedback is important in building your reputation as a seller so customers can be confident buying from. If you followed my advice by at first BUYING some things on Ebay before you started selling, hopefully you received some feedback from those transactions. While it can be tempting to ask or even beg for feedback (nothing makes me cringe more than people BEGGING for feedback), if you are accurate in your listing descriptions and ship out orders promptly and in a professional manner, the feedback will come.

CHAPTER 16

PAYING FEES...AND YOURSELF!

I am guessing you turned to selling on Ebay in order to MAKE money, so it's important to manage your account. However, you also need to keep track of the money you are earning offline so that you'll be prepared when tax season rolls around.

Paying Your Fees: Ebay charges fees when you list items (unless they are running a free listing promotion or you have a plan where you get free listings; for instance, I have an Ebay store and get a certain number of free listings every month) and when you sell items, plus there are also fees for using PayPal.

While the PayPal fees are taken out with each transaction (meaning they come out automatically and you don't have to manually pay them), Ebay keeps a running account total of the fees you incur with them. At the end of the month, they invoice you with the fees you owe.

It is easy to ignore your fees until they are due, but if you are selling a lot of items, your fees can quickly rack up, meaning you will have a large bill to pay. I prefer to keep ahead of fees by paying them as I go, usually every few days. It's easy to make a full or partial payment on your fees; just click on the Account tab in My Ebay; your balance will be there, and you can click on the "Make a One Time Payment" link to pay all or some of the amount.

Dedicated Ebay Bank Account: In addition to setting up a PayPal account, it's also a good idea to get a separate checking account dedicated solely to your business. Having a business account separate from your personal account makes keeping track of business income and expenses so much easier.

If you aren't already a member of a credit union, look for one in your area as they usually offer free account set up, free checking and no ATM fees. You will want to get checks under your business account so that you can buy things such as office supplies directly from your business account. Since I get a lot of shipping supplies at Sam's Club, having a dedicated business checking account is necessary since I don't have the type of credit cards Sam's stores accept.

Having a dedicated credit card for your business is also a good idea. I have a credit card that I keep on file with Ebay to pay any fees that I don't pay before my billing cycle is up. It's on file with PayPal as a back-up payment source in case I have to issue a refund or if I want to buy something myself as I rarely keep funds in my PayPal account.

In the rare instance that I have to take a package to the Post Office for shipping (I do most of my shipping from home), I use the credit card to pay for the postage. I also buy shipping supplies from Staples and order them online from sites such as ValueMailers.com and ULine.com, and I need a credit card to make all of those purchases. And I also use my credit card to buy inventory at thrift stores and even at some estate sales.

Charging these business supplies and services makes it easy to track my expenses. I chose a business credit card that offered rewards, too, so that I get something back for using it. However, be careful to pay off your credit card every month or you'll soon be using all of your profits to pay for fees. When I sold new gift items that I bought at wholesale, I had to order them using a credit card; and the fees definitely added up quickly!

Ebay Accounting System: I keep both a check register and a record of my expenses. Note that keeping a business checking account and a record of your GROSS sales are two different things. My check register shows me exactly how much money I've withdrawn from PayPal along with any checks I've written so that I always know how much actual cash I have in the bank.

However, when tax time rolls around, the IRS needs to know my GROSS sales number. If you sell over $20,000 a year on Ebay, PayPal will send you a tax form. However, even if you don't meet that threshold, you still have to declare your gross sales. Fortunately, you can find your total Ebay sales under the "Performance" tab in your Seller Dashboard.

Separate from my day-to-day check ledger is my record of expenses. While my check ledger is for my own personal use, my record of expenses is for my accountant. Every month, I comb through my checking and credit card statements, along with any records of cash I've spent, to come up with my total expenses for the month. The expenses I track for tax purposes are:

Credit Cards Fees (if you are charging supplies and/or inventory)

Ebay Fees (I pay my Ebay fees as I go, but if you let them accumulate and go onto a credit card, you'll need to account for them every month.)

PayPal Fees (PayPal fees are separate from Ebay fees)

Internet/Phone (my internet connection and my iPhone)

Office Supplies (everything from copy paper to shipping supplies)

Postage (the total postage costs for my business, regardless of whether the buyer pays for shipping or I do)

Cost of Goods (anything I buy to resell)

I also track my monthly **health insurance premiums, doctor co-pays, dentist visits**, and **prescription drug costs**. In addition, I use an app on my iPhone to track **mileage**. And I alert my accountant if I've added in **equipment** to my business, such as a new computer or printer. Since I run my business out of my home, my accountant also factors in how much of my house is used for my business.

At the end of every month, I write down my gross Ebay sales number. I then add up each of my expense columns. At the end of the year, I add up my total gross sales (again, since I sell over $20,000 a year on Ebay, PayPal issues me a tax form with my gross sales total) and each of my categories from each of the 12 months. I then just give my accountant ONE sheet of paper with my yearly TOTALS. I don't have to tell him how much cash I withdrew for my own personal use; for taxes, the IRS needs to know my GROSS SALES and all of my BUSINESS DEDUCTIONS, i.e. my expenses.

While many people use a basic spreadsheet program such as Excel or a simple bookkeeping program from a site like GoDaddy, I actually just type everything up in a Word document. Whether it's on the computer or in a notebook isn't important; what matters is that you are somehow keeping track of your numbers. So, find a system that works best for you and commit to keeping it accurately up-to-date; don't wait until year's end to try to figure out all of your expenses!

Think of your sales and expenses just like the debits and credits on a checkbook ledger. **Debits are your expenses** (withdraws of money) on the check register. **Credits are the funds you earn** (deposits of money) on the check register. From there, each of your debits should fall into one of your expense categories.

Figuring out your **NET versus GROSS** income is KEY to running any business. GROSS is the total amount of money you bring in BEFORE expenses are taken out. After you've accounted for all of your expenses, or "debits", you will have your NET income, which is the actual PROFIT you made. BUT WAIT! It's important to remember that the NET income you are showing after deducting expenses doesn't include taxes. And Americans must account for any income over $600 that they earn from a single source during the course of a year. That's why, if you intend to have a substantial Ebay business, you should consult with an accountant to understand any tax implications you may be facing, especially if you already have another job.

Paying Yourself: One of the questions I get asked a lot are, "How much should I pay myself?" and "How much money should I reinvest in my business?" After all of your business expenses are accounted for and you have your NET income, you will need to decide how much to keep for yourself and how much to put back into your business.

However, with Ebay, your sales, and therefore, your cash flow, can vary wildly; which makes answering these two questions nearly impossible. All I can really do in this instance is share with you how I personally handle this division of paying myself versus reinvesting in my business.

I withdraw my money from PayPal nearly every day, which means I'm constantly updating my check register. I keep my business expenses that I don't pay for with cash or check to one credit card so that they are easy to track. While I will need to report my total gross sales along with my expenses to the IRS at the end of the year, on a day-to-day basis, I'm dealing with actual cash coming in. I have to be aware that even though there is money in my bank account, there are still business expenses to pay for, including taxes.

After I pay my credit card and take out money for my personal expenses, I look at what is left and decide how much to reinvest into my business and if there is any left for me to spend how I wish. If I see that, on average, I'm spending $500 on inventory, I'll likely reserve that much money for sourcing in the next month. What's left is extra money for me to spend as I wish.

However, if sales have been really slow, I may find that after the bills are paid, there isn't much money left. So, I have to make a choice: put it back in my business for supplies and inventory, or put it into my pocket for fun. How much of your Ebay profits you decide to keep for yourself and how much you reinvest into your business is only something you can decide. I'm always thinking ahead to when I know sales will be slow, specifically in the summer. I want to make sure that when I have a good month that I save some of that money back to get me through the slow times. And of course, I am always reminding myself that there will be taxes to be paid on my earnings, too.

You always want to remember that you are selling on Ebay to MAKE money for YOURSELF! Keeping a ledger will help you track your cash flow and expenses so that you can make an informed decision about how much money to take out for you and how much to leave in for your business. Don't get caught in the trap of reinvesting everything you make back into Ebay; be sure to PAY YOURSELF! If you are finding that there is no money left after your expenses have been paid, then you are paying too much for inventory, selling it for too little, or both.

CHAPTER 17

TROUBLESHOOTING

Problems happen all of the time in life, and they happen on Ebay. Here are some tips to help you deal with issues you may encounter when selling on Ebay:

HELP! A customer wants me to end an auction early and sell an item to them for a set price! When you place an item up for auction, you may have someone message you that they will buy the item if you end the auction.

Bottom line: Do NOT do this! People like this are likely trying to low-ball you because they think they can get the item for less than it will go for at auction. When I get messages like this, I simply reply that the auction is already in motion with watchers and that we will not be ending it early. Period!

HELP! A customer claims they haven't received their package, yet tracking shows it was delivered! This comes up every so often, and it's usually a case where someone else in the home has taken in the package or it was delivered to a neighbor. I ask the customer to double check, reminding them that tracking shows it was delivered. Once they know you have tracking (which is why you should always ship through Ebay), you would be amazed at how quickly they find the item! Sadly, there are people out there who try to get full refunds on their orders by saying they haven't arrived.

HELP! A customer says their item arrived broken! When a customer messages me that their item arrived broken, I calmly reply that I am so sorry and ask them to provide me with a photo of the damage. Do NOT just blindly give out refunds; it is important to ask for proof. Ebay has added the ability to attach photos in their messaging system, so it's easy for buyers to send you a picture.

There are scammers out there who break their own item, buy a replacement on Ebay, and then try to pass off their original broken item as the one they just bought. While these scams are few and far between, they do happen.

If you get a picture of an item that is broken, you will have to issue a refund. If you don't, the customer will file a claim with Ebay, and Ebay will automatically refund their money by taking it out of your PayPal account. While this can be frustrating, it is just a part of selling online. And it will make you want to ensure that your orders are packaged to the best of your ability!

HELP! I got an email from Ebay or PayPal saying I need to reset my account/my account has been suspended/I need to provide verification of my identity and to click on a link in the email! Remember that ALL Ebay and PayPal messages go through Ebay's messaging system; you will NEVER get an email from Ebay or PayPal sent directly to your email without a copy of it also being in your Ebay messages. Any email asking for your password or for you to click on a link to take a survey is a SCAM. Ignore it and delete it!

HELP! My listing ended without a sale! Did your item have any watchers? Did anyone ask you questions about it? Take a good look at your listing to see if you can improve on it by writing a better title, including more photos or adding to the description. Maybe your price was too high, or you had it at Auction when it would sell better at Fixed Price. Edit your listing and then relist it with the changes. If it doesn't sell the second time around and it's getting any traffic or watchers, it may be better to just pull it to donate or sell at your own garage sale.

HELP! A customer is threatening to leave me negative feedback if I don't do something and/or they are cursing at me! Feedback extortion is NOT allowed; neither is foul or threatening language. Report messages like this immediately!

CONCULSION

Whether you are just looking to learn about Ebay so that you can sell things now and then, or if you want to make selling on Ebay a part-time or even full-time job, I hope this book has helped you get started! As I mentioned in the Introduction, Ebay is a unique marketplace with its own set of policies and rules.

There is a learning curve to selling on Ebay, but once you get a few sales under your belt, it will become second nature. The main thing is to just get started. If you've never shopped on Ebay before, buy a few items to see how the process works and how other people ship their items. Then try selling some things from around your own house to get the hang of listing and shipping. After a handful of transactions, you'll be on your way to being a confident and experienced Ebay seller!

For more information about selling on Ebay, be sure to check out my other books, all of which are available on Amazon.

ABOUT THE AUTHOR

Ann Eckhart is a writer, blogger, YouTube creator, social media influencer, and Ebay seller based in Iowa. She has numerous Kindle books available on topics including selling on Ebay, saving money, and making money online. For more information, visit her website at AnnEckhart.com.

Printed in Great Britain
by Amazon